MUSIC
MANUSCRIPT BOOK

Valerie Kerr

Order this book online at www.trafford.com
or email orders@trafford.com

Most Trafford titles are also available at major online book retailers.

Printed in the United States of America.

ISBN: 978-1-4669-6288-0 (sc)
ISBN: 978-1-4669-6289-7 (e)

Trafford rev. 10/05/2012

 www.trafford.com

North America & international
toll-free: 1 888 232 4444 (USA & Canada)
phone: 250 383 6864 ♦ fax: 812 355 4082

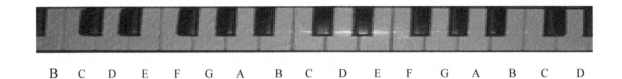

| B | C | D | E | F | G | A | B | C | D | E | F | G | A | B | C | D |

Notice where the **white notes** lie in relation to the **two black note** and **three black note groups**. Allow the **two & three black notes groups** to be your guide to finding your **white note names** quickly and easily.

Treble Stave   (Write your own treble clef then write one octave from Middle C Upwards)

_____
_____
_____
_____
_____

Treble Lines: Rhyme_Every Good Boy Deserves Fruit

Treble Spaces: Rhyme_F A C E spells Face.

Bass Stave   **(Write your own Bass clef then write one octave from Middle C downwards.)**

_____
_____
_____
_____
_____

Bass Line: Rhyme_Good Boys Deserve Fruit Always
Bass Spaces: Rhyme_All Cows Eat Grass

Note Values   Draw your own Semibreve, Minim, Crotchet, Quaver & Semiquaver Notes.

Semibreve (Whole Note)   4 Counts
Minim (Half Note)   2 Counts
Crotchet (Quarter Note)   1 Count
Quaver (Eighth Note)   ½ Count
Semiquaver (Sixteenth Note)   1/4 Count

Dotted Notes are half the value of the note which lies before the dot.
For example a dotted minim has 3 counts.

1

Rest Values:

Draw your own Semibreve, Minim, Crotchet, Quaver & Semiquaver Rests.

Semibreves	4 Counts
Minims	2 Counts
Crotchets	1 Count
Quavers	½ Count
Semiquavers	1/4 Count

Dotted Rests are half the value of the rest which lies before the dot.
For example a dotted minim has 3 counts.

Valerie Kerr
Copyright VKRS.
http://www.musiceducation.co.za
Val@musiceducation.co.za

2

MAJOR & MINOR SCALES

Sharp Scales Major		Sharp Scales Relative minor	
C . . .		A	
G	F#	E	F#
D	F# C#	B	F# C#
A	F# C# G#	F#	F# C# G#
E	F# C# G# D#C#	F#	C# G# D#
B	F# C# G# D# A#	G#	F# C# G# D# A#
F#	F# C# G# D# A# E#	D#	F# C# G# D# A# E#
C#	F# C# G# D# A# E# B#	A#	F# C# G# D# A# E# B#

The Minor scales are known as (Harmonic) and (Melodic) Minors. Each one has the same accidentals as its relative major except for the rule given below.

Harmonic Minor <u>Rule</u>: Has the same accidentals as its relative major except that the 7th Note is raised going up & down)

Melodic Minor <u>Rule</u>: Has the same accidentals as its relative major except 6th & 7th notes are raised going up & 6th & 7th are Lowered coming down (Natural minor)

SCALE MOVEMENT SHOWING:—DEGREE, TONIC SOLFA & TECHNICAL NAMES.

Any scale may be used. C Major is the scale example used.

Scale	Degree	Tonic Solfa	Technical Names
C	1	Doh	Tonic
D	2	Ray	Supertonic
E	3	Me	Mediant
F	4	Fah	Sub Dominant
G	5	Soh	Dominant
A	6	Lah	Sub Mediant
B	7	Te	Leading Note
C	8	Doh	Tonic

TIME SIGNATURES

Simple   Simple time grouping is in Single beats.

The numbers <u>Two, Three or Four</u> appear at the top

TheNumber at the top indicates the number of beats being counted in a bar.

The number at the bottom is the type of note being counted.

For example a 4 at the bottom instructs Crotchets to be counted.

2 at the bottom instructs Minims to be counted.

8 at the bottom instructs Quavers to be counted.

2/4	2 crotchets in a bar	3/4	3 crotchets in a bar	4/4	4 crotchets in a bar
2/8	2 Quavers in a bar	3/8	3 Quavers in a bar	4/8	4 Quavers in a bar
2/2	2 Minims in a bar	3/2	3 Minims in a bar	4/2	4 Minims in a bar

Compound   Compound time grouping is in Dotted beats. The numbers <u>Six, Nine or Twelve</u> appear at the top.

6/8	6 Quavers in a bar	9/8	9 Quavers in a bar	12/8	12 Quavers in a bar
6/4	6 crotchets in a bar	9/4	9 crotchets in a bar	12/4	12 crotchets in a bar
6/2	6 Minims in a bar	9/2	9 Minims in a bar	12/2	12 Minims in a bar

Printed in the United States
By Bookmasters